'Faith is trusting, trusting wholly upon the person, work, merit, and power of the Son of God.' And again, 'Faith is the linen which binds the plaster of Christ's reconciliation to the sore of our sin.' Or when looking at how people try to avoid faith, Spurgeon noted, 'Doubts are as plentiful as blackberries, and all hands and lips are stained with them.' With such deep and profound simplicity, Spurgeon adorns every page of this evangelistic booklet. *In Around the Wicket Gate* Spurgeon takes the role of John Bunyan's famous evangelist and pleads with sinners to 'Flee from the wrath to come' and assures them of the absolute sufficiency of Christ in his person and work and the impeccable trustworthiness of his word. Chapter seven on the sufferings of Christ—both in body and in soul—closes with theological propositions built on Toplady's 'Whence This Fear and Unbelief.' It is profoundly moving and seals the truth of the certainty of salvation through Christ and Christ alone. Read this book for your own edification and give it to a lost friend for a clear explanation of the gospel and an earnest and friendly appeal to believe.

Tom Nettles
Senior Professor of Historical Theology,
The Southern Baptist Theological Seminary, Louisville, Kentucky

This book is one of the most famous books that the kind, loving, extraordinary Christian, Charles Haddon Spurgeon, ever wrote. If you are just mildly interested in what is a Christian and how people become followers of Jesus Christ, then there is simply no more straightforward and fascinating book for you to read but this.

Geoff Thomas
Conference Speaker and author, Aberystwyth, Wales

If you grew up with a vague familiarity with Christianity, but it never meant much to you, read this book. Like no one else, Spurgeon lays out the simplicity, the power and the truth of the good news of Jesus. This classic gospel appeal is a model for Christian evangelism, and it may be life-changing for you.

John Folmar
Senior Pastor, United Christian Church of Dubai

This little gem of a book combines razor-sharp spiritual diagnoses, timeless and helpful illustrations, and a clear route back to Jesus Christ as the only source of personal freedom, forgiveness and future hope. Not only will those seeking after truth be helped by this book, those who share the good news of hope in Christ Jesus will be equipped to clear the clutter from people's minds and point them to the Saviour.

Alasdair MacLeod
Senior Minister, Smithton Free Church, Inverness

Re-reading Around the Wicket Gate brought back to mind the moment that both my wife and I trusted in Jesus for salvation – together!

We had been invited to church by a friend and the word preached had a powerful and profound effect on us both. But it was later through reading this book that we came to trust in Jesus, by simply accepting the gift of salvation.

I hope this little book will be used again by the Lord to bring many others to himself.

Iain MacAskill
Minister, Free Church of Scotland, Stirling, Scotland

AROUND *the* WICKET GATE

**Help for Those Who Only
Know *About* Christ**

C. H. SPURGEON

CHRISTIAN
HERITAGE

Copyright © Christian Focus Publications

ISBN 978-1-5271-0341-2

10 9 8 7 6 5 4 3 2 1

This edition published in 2019
in the
Christian Heritage Imprint
by
Christian Focus Publications Ltd.,
Geanies House, Fearn, Ross-shire,
IV20 1TW, Great Britain

www.christianfocus.com

Cover design by Daniel Van Straaten

Printed by Gutenberg, Malta

CONTENTS

FOREWORD

The renowned Reformed Baptist preacher, Charles Haddon Spurgeon (1834-1892) is arguably the greatest pastor-evangelist that God has ever given to the church. Known as the undisputed 'Prince of Preachers,' this stalwart of the faith is easily the most beloved expounder of Scripture that we have witnessed over the last twenty centuries. Of the many superlatives that could be said of him, the greatest accolade was his unquenchable fire in proclaiming the gospel with contagious zeal. Simply put, Spurgeon was, first and foremost, a harvester of souls.

No man ever stood in one pulpit for almost four decades and preached the saving message of Jesus Christ with such far-reaching success. His famed pulpit at the Metropolitan Tabernacle in London became the launching pad for his global outreach that stretched across oceans and around the world. By this public ministry, Spurgeon has become the gold standard in evangelistic preaching for the past century.

Not only was Spurgeon a prolific preacher, he was also a skilled author, who affected untold millions with his writings. He edited his weekly sermons, which were sold on the streets of London and throughout the United Kingdom as the 'Penny Pulpit.' In addition, he wrote many books that were purchased in voluminous numbers. Among his works was *The Soul Winner*, written to believers, urging them to bear witness of the Lord Jesus Christ to a lost and perishing world. Spurgeon remains to this day the most widely read Christian author in history.

One of the more effective works to come from the pen of Spurgeon is the book that you presently hold in your hand, *Around the Wicket Gate*. The phrase 'the wicket gate' had been popularized by John Bunyan in his all-time classic, *The Pilgrim's Progress*. Bunyan drew from the imagery used by Jesus in the Sermon on the Mount when He called out to the unconverted, 'Enter through the narrow gate' (Matt. 7:13, NIV). Spurgeon developed his book around this simple metaphor of the gate as he wrote this evangelistic tool. It is directed toward those who are near the kingdom of God, but who have not yet entered it.

Spurgeon rightly observed that many people are near the wicket gate, but have not come through it by faith. They have admired the beauty of the narrow gate, which is Jesus Christ Himself. They have watched others step through this gate. They have learned many fascinating truths about the gate. They have taken steps to draw close to the gate. Their toes are even pressing against the gate. But they have not yet taken that final, decisive step of faith to proceed through the gate and into the kingdom of God.

This book was written by Spurgeon to urge searchers to come all the way to saving faith in Jesus Christ. He answers the most common excuses of those who hesitate to enter through the gate. These often raised objections cause countless people to remain outside the gate, perishing in the barren wilderness of indecision. Tragically, these weary souls halt between two opinions and remain uncommitted and, thus, unconverted.

With his brilliantly astute mind, Spurgeon rebuttals the many lame arguments that could be raised by unbelievers that keep them from making this vital decision to believe in Jesus Christ. In addressing those so close to the kingdom of God, but who have not yet entered it, Spurgeon warns that to be *almost* saved is to be altogether lost.

This book is a must-read for all who linger outside the gate. I wonder if this could describe *you*? Could it be that you still find yourself outside the kingdom? Maybe you have heard much about Jesus Christ, but you have not yet committed your life to Him. Are you a stranger to grace? Why do you procrastinate entrusting your life and soul to Him? What holds you back? Spurgeon addresses each of these concerns.

If this describes where you are, it is by no accident that you hold this priceless book in your hands. This treasure, written by Spurgeon, was designed especially for you. It has your name written on it. This book is yet another evidence of the mercy of God that continues to reach out to your lost soul in order that you would be saved. Here is the goodness of God that still pursues you and speaks the truth to you.

This book is also a must-read for those who have already entered into the kingdom of God. It is the responsibility of all believers to witness the gospel of Jesus Christ to those who are lost. In these pages, Spurgeon will better equip you concerning how to engage those who are yet undecided for Christ. Here you will find the wisdom you need for your own evangelistic efforts to win others to Christ. Here you will be taught how to answer the many excuses offered by those who have not yet believed.

In these chapters, I want to remind you that you are reading the writings of perhaps the most skilled evangelist ever to take pen in hand and write to those who are without Christ. If you have not yet believed in Him, may the Lord use this book to lead you to enter through the narrow gate. And if you have already believed upon Him, may God use this resource to better prepare you for fruitful evangelistic endeavors in His vineyard.

STEVEN J. LAWSON
President, OnePassion Ministries,
Dallas, Texas

Preface

Millions of men are in the outlying regions, far off from God and peace; for these we pray, and to these we give warning. But just now we have to do with a smaller company, who are not far from the kingdom, but have come right up to the wicket gate which stands at the head of the way of life. One would think that they would hasten to enter, for a free and open invitation is placed over the entrance, the porter waits to welcome them, and there is but this one way to eternal life. He that is most loaded seems the most likely to pass in and begin the heavenward journey; but what ails the other men?

This is what I want to find out. Poor fellows! They have come a long way already to get where they are; and the King's highway, which they seek, is right before them: why do they not take to the Pilgrim Road at once? Alas! they have a great many reasons; and foolish as those reasons are, it needs a very wise man to answer them all. I cannot pretend to do so. Only the Lord Himself can remove the folly which is bound up in their hearts, and lead them to take the great decisive step. Yet the Lord works by means; and I have prepared this little book in the earnest hope that He may work by it to the blessed end of leading seekers to an immediate, simple trust in the Lord Jesus.

He who does not take the step of faith, and so enter upon the road to heaven, will perish. It will be an awful thing to die just outside the gate of life. Almost saved, but altogether lost! This is the most terrible of positions. A man just outside Noah's ark would have been drowned; a manslayer close to the wall of the city of refuge, but yet outside of it, would be slain; and the man who is within a yard of Christ, and yet has not trusted Him, will be lost. Therefore am I in terrible earnest to get my hesitating friends over the threshold. *Come in! Come in!* is my pressing entreaty. *'Wherefore standest thou without?'* is my solemn enquiry. May the Holy Spirit render my pleadings effectual with many who shall glance at these pages! May He cause His own Almighty power to create faith in the soul at once!

My reader, if God blesses this book to you, do the writer this favour – either lend your own copy to one who is lingering at the gate, or buy another and give it away; for his great desire is that this little volume should be of service to many thousands of souls.

To God this book is commended; for without His grace nothing will come of all that is written.

C. H. SPURGEON

1
AWAKENING

Great numbers of persons have no concern about eternal things. They care more about their cats and dogs than about their souls. It is a great mercy to be made to think about ourselves, and how we stand towards God and the eternal world. This is full often a sign that salvation is coming to us. By nature we do not like the anxiety which spiritual concern causes us, and we try, like sluggards, to sleep again. This is great foolishness; for it is at our peril that we trifle when death is so near, and judgment is so sure. If the Lord has chosen us to eternal life, he will not let us return to our slumber. If we are sensible, we shall pray that our anxiety about our souls may never come to an end till we are really and truly saved. Let us say from our hearts:

He that suffered in my stead,
Shall my Physician be;
I will not be comforted
Till Jesus comfort me.

It would be an awful thing to go dreaming down to hell, and there to lift up our eyes with a great gulf fixed between us and heaven. It will be equally terrible to be aroused to escape from the wrath to come, and then to shake off the warning influence, and go back to our insensibility. I notice that those who overcome their convictions and continue in their sins are not so easily moved the next time: every awakening which is thrown away leaves the soul more drowsy than before, and less likely to be again stirred to holy feeling. Therefore our heart should be greatly troubled at the thought of getting rid of its trouble in any other than the right way. One who had the gout was cured of it by a quack medicine, which drove the disease within, and the patient died. To be cured of distress of mind by a false hope, would be a terrible business: the remedy would be worse than the disease. Better far that our tenderness of conscience should cause us long years of anguish, than that we should lose it, and perish in the hardness of our hearts.

Yet awakening is not a thing to rest in, or to desire to have lengthened out month after month. If I start up in a fright, and find my house on fire, I do not sit down at the edge of the bed, and say to myself, 'I hope I am truly awakened! Indeed, I am deeply grateful that I am not left to sleep on!' No, I want to escape from threatened death, and so I hasten to the door or to the window, that I may get out, and may not perish where I am. It would be a questionable boon to be aroused, and yet not to escape from the danger. Remember, awakening is not salvation. A man may know that he is lost, and yet he may never be saved. He may be made thoughtful, and yet he may die in his sins. If you find out that you are bankrupt, the consideration of your debts will not pay them. A man may examine his wounds all the year around, and they will be none the nearer being healed because he feels their smart, and notes their number. It is one trick of the devil to tempt a man to be satisfied with a sense of sin; and another trick of the same deceiver to insinuate that the sinner may not be content to trust Christ, unless he can bring a certain measure of despair to add to the Saviour's finished work. Our awakenings are not to help the Saviour, but to help us to the Saviour. To imagine that my feeling of sin is to assist in the removal of the sin is absurd. It is as though I said that water could not cleanse my face unless I had looked longer in the glass, and had counted the smuts upon my forehead. A sense of need of salvation by grace is a very healthful sign; but one needs wisdom to use it aright, and not to make an idol of it.

Some seem as if they had fallen in love with their doubts, and fears, and distresses. You cannot get them away from their terrors – they seem wedded to them. It is said that the worst trouble with horses when their stables are on fire, is that you cannot get them to come out of their stalls. If they would but follow your lead, they might escape the flames; but they seem to be paralysed with fear. So the fear of the fire prevents their escaping the fire. Reader, will your very fear of the wrath to come prevent your escaping from it? We hope not.

One who had been long in prison was not willing to come out. The door was open; but he pleaded even with tears to be allowed to stay where he had been so long. Fond of prison! Wedded to the iron bolts and the prison fare! Surely the prisoner must have been a little touched in the head! Are you willing to remain an awakened one, and nothing more? Are you not eager to be at once forgiven? If you would tarry in anguish and dread, surely you, too, must be a little out of your mind! If peace is to be had, have it at once! Why tarry in the darkness of the pit, wherein your feet sink in the miry clay? There is light to be had; light marvellous and heavenly; why lie in the gloom and die in anguish? You do not know how near salvation is to you. If you did, you would surely stretch out your hand and take it, for there it is; and *it is to be had for the taking.*

Do not think that feelings of despair would fit you for mercy. When the pilgrim, on his way to the Wicket Gate, tumbled into the Slough of Despond, do you think that, when the foul mire of that slough stuck to his garments, it was a recommendation to him, to get him easier admission at the head of the way? It is not so. The pilgrim did not think so by any means: neither may you. It is not what *you* feel that will save you, but what *Jesus* felt. Even if there were some healing value in feelings, they would have to be good ones; and the feeling which makes us doubt the power of Christ to save, and prevents our finding salvation in him, is by no means a good one, but a cruel wrong to the love of Jesus.

Our friend has come to see us, and has travelled through our crowded London by rail, or tram, or omnibus. On a sudden he turns pale. We ask him what is the matter, and he answers, 'I have lost my pocket-book, and it contained all the money I have in the world'. He goes over the amount to a penny, and describes the cheques, bills, notes, and coins. We tell him that it must be a great consolation to him to be so accurately acquainted with the extent of his loss.

He does not seem to see the worth of our consolation. We assure him that he ought to be grateful that he has so clear a sense of his loss; for many persons might have lost their pocket-books and have been quite unable to compute their losses. Our friend is not, however, cheered in the least. 'No,' says he, 'to know my loss does not help me to recover it. Tell me where I can find my property, and you have done me real service; but merely to know my loss is no comfort whatever.' Even so, to believe that you have sinned, and that your soul is forfeited to the justice of God, is a very proper thing; but it will not save. Salvation is not by our knowing our own ruin, but by fully grasping the deliverance provided in Christ Jesus. A person who refuses to look to the Lord Jesus, but persists in dwelling upon his sin and ruin, reminds us of a boy who dropped a shilling down an open grating of a London sewer, and lingered there for hours, finding comfort in saying, 'It rolled in just there! Just between those two iron bars I saw it go right down.' Poor soul! Long might he remember the details of his loss before he would in this way get back a single penny into his pocket, wherewith to buy himself a piece of bread. You see the drift of the parable; profit by it.

2
JESUS ONLY

We cannot too often or too plainly tell the seeking soul that his only hope for salvation lies in the Lord Jesus Christ. It lies in Him completely, only, and alone. To save both from the guilt and the power of sin, Jesus is all-sufficient. His name is called Jesus, because 'He shall save His people from their sins' (Matt 1:21). 'The Son of man hath power on earth to forgive sins' (Matt. 9:6). He is exalted on high 'to give repentance and remission of sins' (see Acts 5:31). It pleased God from of old to devise a method of salvation which should be all contained in His only-begotten Son. The Lord Jesus, for the working out of this salvation, became man, and being found in fashion as a man, became obedient to death, even the death of the cross. If another way of deliverance had been possible, the cup of bitterness would have passed from Him. It stands to reason that the darling of heaven would not have died to save us if we could have been rescued at less expense. Infinite grace provided the great sacrifice; infinite love submitted to death for our sakes. How can we dream that there can be another way than the way which God has provided at such cost, and set forth in Holy Scripture so simply and so pressingly? Surely it is true that 'Neither is there salvation in any other: for there is none other name under heaven given among men, whereby we must be saved' (Acts 4:12).

To suppose that the Lord Jesus has only half saved men, and that there is needed some work or feeling of their own to finish His work, is wicked. What is there of ours that could be added to His blood and righteousness? 'All our righteousnesses are as filthy rags' (Isa. 64:6). Can these be patched on to the costly fabric of His divine righteousness? Rags and fine white linen! Our dross and His pure gold! It is an insult to the Saviour to dream of such a thing. We have sinned enough, without adding this to all our other offences.

Even if we had any righteousness in which we could boast; if our fig leaves were broader than usual, and were not so utterly fading, it would be wisdom to put them away, and accept that righteousness which must be far more pleasing to God than anything of our own. The Lord must see more that is acceptable in His Son than in the best of us. *The best of us!* The words seem satirical, though they were not so intended. What best is there about any of us? 'There is none that doeth good; no, not one' (Ps. 14:3). I who write these lines, would most freely confess that I have not a thread of goodness of my own. I could not make up so much as a rag, or a piece of a rag. I am utterly destitute. But if I had the fairest suit of good works which even pride can imagine, I would tear it up that I might put on nothing but the garments of salvation, which are freely given by the Lord Jesus, out of the heavenly wardrobe of His own merits.

It is most glorifying to our Lord Jesus Christ that we should hope for every good thing from Him alone. This is to treat Him as He deserves to be treated; for as He is God, and beside Him there is none else, we are bound to look unto Him and be saved.

This is to treat Him as He loves to be treated, for He bids all those who labour and are heavy laden to come to Him, and He will give them rest. To imagine that He cannot save to the uttermost is to limit the Holy One of Israel, and put a slur upon His power; or else to slander the loving heart of the Friend of sinners, and cast a doubt upon His love. In either case, we should commit a cruel and wanton sin against the tenderest points of His honour, which are His ability and willingness to save all that come unto God by Him.

The child, in danger of the fire, just clings to the fireman, and trusts to him alone. She raises no question about the strength of his limbs to carry her, or the zeal of his heart to rescue her; but she clings. The heat is terrible, the smoke is blinding, but she clings; and her deliverer quickly bears her to safety. In the same childlike confidence cling to Jesus, who can and will bear you out of danger from the flames of sin.

The nature of the Lord Jesus should inspire us with the fullest confidence. As He is God, He is almighty to save; as He is man, He is filled with all fulness to bless; as He is God and man in one Majestic Person, He meets man in His creatureship and God in His holiness. The ladder is long enough to reach from Jacob prostrate on the earth, to Jehovah reigning in heaven. To bring another ladder would be to suppose that He failed to bridge the distance; and this would be grievously to dishonour Him. If even to add to His words is to draw a curse upon ourselves, what must it be to pretend to add to Himself? Remember that He, Himself, is the Way; and to suppose that we must, in some manner, add to the divine road, is to be arrogant enough to think of adding to Him. Away with such a notion! Loathe it as you would blasphemy against the Lord of love.

To come to Jesus with a price in our hand, would be insufferable pride, even if we had any price that we could bring. What does He need of us? What could we bring if He did need it? Would He sell the priceless blessings of His redemption? That which He wrought out in His heart's blood, would He barter it with us for tears, and vows, or for ceremonial observances, and feelings, and works? He is not reduced to make a market of Himself: He will give freely, as beseems His royal love; but He that offereth a price to Him knows not with whom he is dealing, nor how grievously he vexes His free Spirit. Empty-handed sinners may have what they will. All that they can possibly need is in Jesus, and He gives it for the asking; but we must believe that He is all in all, and we must not dare to breathe a word about completing what He has finished, or fitting ourselves for what He gives to us as undeserving sinners.

The reason why we may hope for forgiveness of sin, and life eternal, by faith in the Lord Jesus, is that God has so appointed. He has pledged Himself in the gospel to save all who truly trust in the Lord Jesus, and He will never run back from His promise. He is so well pleased with His only-begotten Son, that He takes pleasure in all who lay hold upon Him as their one and only hope. The great God Himself has taken hold on him who has taken hold on His Son. He works salvation for all who look for that salvation to the once-slain Redeemer. For the honour of His Son, He will not suffer the man who trusts in Him to be ashamed. 'He that believeth on the Son hath everlasting life' (John 3:36); for the ever-living God has taken him unto Himself, and has given to him to be a partaker of His life. If Jesus only be your trust, you need not fear but that you shall effectually be saved, both now and in the day of His appearing.

When a man confides, there is a point of union between him and God, and that union guarantees blessing. Faith saves us because it makes us cling to Christ Jesus, and He is one with God, and thus brings us into connection with

God. I am told that, years ago, above the Falls of Nia-
gara, a boat was upset, and two men were being carried
down by the current, when persons on the shore managed
to float a rope out to them, which rope was seized by them
both. One of them held fast to it, and was safely drawn to
the bank but the other, seeing a great log come floating
by, unwisely let go the rope, and clung to the great piece
of timber, for it was the bigger thing of the two, and ap-
parently better to cling to. Alas! the timber, with the man
on it, went right over the vast abyss, because there was
no union between the wood and the shore. The size of
the log was no benefit to him who grasped it; it needed a
connection with the shore to produce safety. So, when a
man trusts to his works, or to his prayers, or almsgivings,
or to sacraments, or to anything of that sort, he will not be
saved, because there is no junction between him and God
through Christ Jesus; but faith, though it may seem to be
like a slender cord, is in the hand of the great God on the
shore side; infinite power pulls in the connecting line, and
thus draws the man from destruction. Oh, the blessedness
of faith, because it unites us to God by the Saviour, whom
He has appointed, even Jesus Christ! O reader, is there
not common sense in this matter? Think it over, and may
there soon be a band of union between you and God,
through your faith in Christ Jesus!

3

PERSONAL FAITH IN JESUS

There is a wretched tendency among men to leave Christ Himself out of the gospel. They might as well leave flour out of bread. Men hear the way of salvation explained, and consent to it as being Scriptural, and in every way such as suits their case; but they forget that a plan is of no service unless it is carried out; and that in the matter of salvation their own personal faith in the Lord Jesus is essential. A road to York will not take me there, I must travel along it for myself. All the sound doctrine that ever was believed will never save a man unless he puts his trust in the Lord Jesus for himself.

Mr Macdonald asked the inhabitants of the island of St Kilda how a man must be saved. An old man replied, 'We shall be saved if we repent, and forsake our sins, and turn to God'. 'Yes,' said a middle-aged female, 'and with a true heart too.' 'Ay,' rejoined a third, 'and with prayer'; and, added a fourth, 'It must be the prayer of the heart.' 'And we must be diligent too,' said a fifth, 'in keeping the commandments.' Thus, each having contributed his mite, feeling that a very decent creed had been made up, they all looked and listened for the preacher's approbation; but they had aroused his deepest pity: he had to begin at the beginning, and preach Christ to them. The carnal mind always maps out for itself a way in which self can work and become great; but the Lord's way is quite the reverse. The Lord Jesus puts it very compactly in Mark 16:16: 'He that believeth and is baptised shall be saved.' Believing and being baptised are no matters of merit to be gloried in; they are so simple that boasting is excluded, and free grace bears the palm. This way of salvation is chosen that it might be seen to be of grace alone. It may be that the reader is unsaved: what is the reason? Do you think the way of salvation, as laid down in the text we have quoted, to be dubious? Do you fear that you would not be saved if you followed it? How can that be, when God has pledged His own word for its certainty? How can that fail which God prescribes, and concerning which He gives a promise? Do you think it very easy? Why, then, do you not attend to it? Its ease leaves those without excuse who neglect it. If you would have done some great thing, be not so foolish as to neglect the little thing. To believe is to trust, or lean upon Christ Jesus; in other words, to give up self-reliance, and to rely upon the Lord Jesus. To be baptised is to submit to the ordinance which our Lord fulfilled at Jordan, to which the converted ones submitted at Pentecost, to which the jailer yielded obedience on the very night of his conversion. It is the outward confession which should always go with inward faith. The outward sign saves not; but it sets forth to us our death, burial, and resurrection with Jesus, and, like the Lord's Supper, it is not to be neglected.

The great point is to believe in Jesus, and confess your faith. Do you believe in Jesus? Then, dear friend, dismiss your fears; you shall be saved. Are you still an unbeliever?

Then remember, there is but one door, and if you will not enter by it, you must perish in your sins. The door is there; but unless you enter by it, what is the use of it to you? It is of necessity that you obey the command of the gospel. Nothing can save you if you do not hear the voice of Jesus, and do His bidding indeed and of a truth. Thinking and resolving will not answer the purpose; you must come to real business; for only as you actually believe will you truly live unto God.

I heard of a friend who deeply desired to be the means of the conversion of a young man, and one said to him, 'You may go to him, and talk to him, but you will get him no further; for he is exceedingly well acquainted with the plan of salvation'. It was eminently so; and therefore, when our friend began to speak with the young man, he received for an answer, 'I am much obliged to you, but I do not know that you can tell me much, for I have long known and admired the plan of salvation by the substitutionary sacrifice of Christ'. Alas! he was resting *in*

the plan, but he had not believed *in the Person*. The plan of salvation is most blessed, but it can avail us nothing unless we personally believe in the Lord Jesus Christ Himself. What is the comfort of a plan of a house if you do not enter the house itself? The man in our cut, who is sitting out in the rain, is not deriving much comfort from the plans that are spread out before him. What is the comfort of a plan of clothing if you have not a rag to cover you? Have you never heard of the Arab chief at Cairo, who was very ill, and went to the missionary, and the missionary said he could give him a prescription? He did so; and a week after he found the Arab none the better. 'Did you take my prescription?' he asked. 'Yes, I ate every morsel of the paper.' He dreamed that he was going to be cured by devouring the physician's writing, which I may call the plan of the medicine. He should have had the prescription made up, and then it might have wrought him good, if he had taken the draught: it could do him no good to swallow the recipe. So is it with salvation: it is not the plan of salvation which can save, it is the carrying out of that plan by the Lord Jesus in His death on our behalf, and our acceptance of the same. Under the Jewish law, the offerer brought a bullock, and laid his hands upon it: it was no dream, or theory, or plan. In the victim for sacrifice he found something substantial, which he could handle and touch: even so do we lean upon the real and true work of Jesus, the most substantial thing under heaven. We come to the Lord Jesus by faith, and say, 'God has provided an atonement here, and I accept it. I believe in the fact accomplished on the cross; I am confident that sin was put away by Christ, and I rest on Him'. If you would be saved, you must get beyond the acceptance of plans and doctrines to a resting in the divine person and finished work of the Lord Jesus Christ. Dear reader, will you have Christ now?

Jesus invites all those who labour and are heavy laden to come to Him, and He will give them rest. He does not promise this to their merely dreaming about Him. They must *come*; and they must come *to Him*, and not merely to the Church, to baptism, or to the orthodox faith, or to anything short of His divine person. When the brazen serpent was lifted up in the wilderness, the people were not to look to Moses, nor to the Tabernacle, nor to the pillar of cloud, but to the brazen serpent itself. Looking was not enough unless they looked to the right object: and the right object was not enough unless they looked. It was not enough for them to know about the serpent of brass; they must each one look to it for himself. When a man is ill, he may have a good knowledge of medicine, and yet he may die if he does not actually take the healing draught. We must receive Jesus; for 'to as many as received Him, to them gave He power to become the sons of God' (John 1:12). Lay the emphasis on two words: *We must receive HIM*, and *we must RECEIVE Him*. We must open wide the door, and take Christ Jesus in; for 'Christ in you' is 'the hope of glory' (see Col. 1:27). Christ must be no myth, no dream, no phantom to us, but a real man, and truly God; and our reception of Him must be no forced and feigned acceptance, but the hearty and happy assent and consent of the soul that He shall be the all in all of our salvation.

Will we not at once come to Him, and make Him our sole trust?

The dove is hunted by the hawk, and finds no security from its restless enemy. It has learned that there is shelter for it in the cleft of the rock, and it hastens there with gladsome wing. Once wholly sheltered within its refuge, it fears no bird of prey. But if it did not hide itself in the rock, it would be seized upon by its adversary. The rock would be of no use to the dove, if the dove did not enter its cleft. The whole body must be hidden in the rock. What if ten thousand other birds found a fortress there, yet that fact would not save the one dove which is now pursued by the hawk! It must put its whole self into the shelter, and bury itself within its refuge, or its life will be forfeited to the destroyer.

What a picture of faith is this! It is entering into Jesus, hiding in His wounds.

Rock of Ages, cleft for me.
Let me hide myself in Thee.

The dove is out of sight: the rock alone is seen. So does the guilty soul dart into the riven side of Jesus by faith, and is buried in Him out of sight of avenging justice. But there must be this personal application to Jesus for shelter; and this it is that so many put off from day to day, till it is to be feared that they will 'die in their sins' (see Ezek. 3:19). What an awful word is that! It is what our Lord said to the unbelieving Jews; and He says the same to us at this hour: 'If ye believe not that I am He, ye shall die in your sins' (John 8:24). It makes one's heart to quiver to think that even one who shall read these lines may yet be of the miserable company who will thus perish. The Lord prevent it of His great grace!

I saw, the other day, a remarkable picture, which I shall use as an illustration of the way of salvation by faith in Jesus. An offender had committed a crime for which he must die, but it was in the olden time, when churches were considered to be sanctuaries in which criminals might hide themselves, and so escape from death. See the transgressor! He rushes towards the church, the guards pursue him with their drawn swords, athirst for his blood! They follow him even to the church door. He rushes up the steps, and just as they are about to overtake him, and hew him in pieces on the threshold of the church, out comes the Bishop, and holding up the cross, he cries, 'Back, back! Stain not the precincts of God's house with blood! Stand back!' The fierce soldiers at once respect the emblem, and retire, while the poor fugitive hides himself behind the robes of the Bishop. It is even so with Christ. The guilty sinner flies straight away to Jesus; and though Justice pursues him, Christ lifts up His wounded hands, and cries to Justice, 'Stand back! I shelter this sinner; in the secret place of my tabernacle do I hide him; I will not suffer him to perish, for he puts his trust in Me.' Sinner, fly to Christ! But you answer, 'I am too vile'. The viler you are, the more will you honour Him by believing that He is able to protect even you. 'But I am so great a sinner.' Then the more honour shall be given to Him if you have faith to confide in Him, great sinner though you are. If you have a little sickness, and you tell your physician – 'Sir, I am quite confident in your skill to heal,' there is no compliment in your declaration. Anybody can cure a finger-ache, or a trifling sickness. But if you are sore sick with a complication of diseases which grievously torment you, and you say – 'Sir, I seek no better physician; I will ask no other advice but yours; I trust myself joyfully with you', what an honour have you conferred on him, that you can trust your life in his hands while it is in extreme and immediate danger! Do the like with Christ; put your soul into His care: do it deliberately, and without a doubt. Dare to quit all other hopes: venture all on Jesus; I say 'venture' though there is nothing really venturesome in it, for He is abundantly able to save. Cast yourself simply on Jesus; let nothing but faith be in your soul towards Jesus; believe Him, and trust in Him, and you shall never be made ashamed of your confidence. 'He that believeth on Him shall not be confounded' (1 Pet. 2:6).

4
FAITH VERY SIMPLE

To many, faith seems a hard thing. The truth is, *it is only hard because it is easy*. Naaman thought it hard that he should have to wash in Jordan; but if it had been some great thing, he would have done it right cheerfully. People think that salvation must be the result of some act or feeling, very mysterious, and very difficult; but God's thoughts are not our thoughts, neither are His ways our ways. In order that the feeblest and the most ignorant may be saved, He has made the way of salvation as easy as the A, B, C. There is nothing about it to puzzle anyone; only, as everybody expects to be puzzled by it, many are quite bewildered when they find it to be so exceedingly simple.

The fact is, we do not believe that God means what He is saying; we act as if it could not be true.

I have heard of a Sunday-school teacher who performed an experiment which I do not think I shall ever try with children, for it might turn out to be a very expensive one. Indeed, I feel sure that the result in my case would be very different from what I now describe. This teacher had been trying to illustrate what faith was, and, as he could not get it into the minds of his boys, he took his watch, and said, 'Now, I will give you this watch, John. Will you have it?' John fell thinking what the teacher could mean, and did not seize the treasure, but made no answer. The teach-

er said to the next boy, 'Henry, here is the watch. Will you have it?' The boy, with a very proper modesty, replied, 'No, thank you, sir'. The teacher tried several of the boys with the same result; till at last a youngster, who was not so wise or so thoughtful as the others, but rather more believing, said in the most natural way, 'Thank you, sir,' and put the watch into his pocket. Then the other boys woke up to a startling fact: their companion had received a watch which they had refused. One of the boys quickly asked of the teacher, 'Is he to keep it?'. 'Of course he is,' said the teacher, 'I offered it to him, and he accepted it. I would not give a thing and take a thing: that would be very foolish. I put the watch before you, and said that I gave it to you, but none of you would have it.' 'Oh!' said the boy, 'if I had known you meant it, I would have had it.' Of course he would. He thought it was a piece of acting, and nothing more. All the other boys were in a dreadful state of mind to think that they had lost the watch. Each one cried, 'Teacher, I did not know you meant it, *but I thought* –'. No one took the gift; but every one *thought*. Each one had his theory, except the simple-minded boy who believed what he was told, and got the watch. Now I wish that I could always be such a simple child as literally to believe what the Lord says, and take what He puts before me, resting quite content that He is not playing with me, and that I cannot be wrong in accepting what He sets before me in the gospel. Happy should we be if we would trust, and raise no questions of any sort. But, alas! we will get thinking and doubting. When the Lord uplifts His dear Son before a sinner, that sinner should take Him without hesitation. If you take Him, you have Him; and none can take Him from you. Out with your hand, man, and take Him at once!

When enquirers accept the Bible as literally true, and see that Jesus is really given to all who trust Him, all the difficulty about understanding the way of salvation vanishes like the morning's frost at the rising of the sun.

Two enquiring ones came to me in my vestry. They had been hearing the gospel from me for only a short season, but they had been deeply impressed by it. They expressed their regret that they were about to remove far away, but they added their gratitude that they had heard me at all. I was cheered by their kind thanks, but felt anxious that a more effectual work should be wrought in them, and therefore I asked them, 'Have you in very deed believed in the Lord Jesus Christ? Are you saved?' One of them replied, 'I have been trying hard to believe.' This statement I have often heard, but I will never let it go by me unchallenged. 'No,' I said, 'that will not do. Did you ever tell your father that you tried to believe in him?' After I had dwelt a while upon the matter, they admitted that such language would have been an insult to their father. I then set the gospel very plainly before them in as simple language as I could, and begged them to believe in Jesus, who is more worthy of faith than the best of fathers. One of them replied, 'I cannot realise it: I cannot realise that I am saved.' Then I went on to say, 'God bears testimony to His Son, that whosoever trusts in His Son is saved. Will you make him a liar now, or will you believe His Word?' While I thus spoke, one of them started as if astonished, and she startled us all as she cried, 'O sir, I see it all; I am saved! Oh, do bless Jesus for me; He has shown me the way, and He has saved me! I see it all.' The esteemed sister who had brought these young friends to me knelt down with them while, with all our hearts, we blessed and magnified the Lord for a soul brought into the light. One of the two sisters, however, could not see the gospel as the other had done, though I feel sure she will do so before long. Did it not seem strange that, both hearing the same words, one should come out into clear light, and the other should remain in the gloom? The change which comes over the heart when the understanding grasps the gospel is often reflected in the face, and shines there like the light of heaven. Such newly enlightened souls often exclaim, 'Why, sir, it is so plain; how is it I have not seen it before this? I understand all I have read in the Bible now, though I could not make it out before. It has all come in a minute, and now I see what I could never understand before.' The fact is, the truth was always plain, but they were looking for signs and wonders, and therefore did not see what was nigh them. Old men often look for their spectacles when they are on their foreheads; and it is commonly observed that we fail to see that which is straight before us. Christ Jesus is before our faces, and we have only to look to Him, and live; but we make all manner of bewilderment of it, and so manufacture a maze out of that which is plain as a pikestaff.

The little incident about the two sisters reminds me of another. A much-esteemed friend came to me one Sabbath morning after service, to shake hands with me, 'for,' said she, 'I was fifty years old on the same day as yourself. I am like you in that one thing, sir; but I am the very reverse of you in better things.' I remarked, 'Then you must be a very good woman; for in many things I wish I also could be the reverse of what I am.' 'No, no,' she said, 'I did not mean anything of that sort: I am not right at all.' 'What!' I cried, 'are you not a believer in the Lord Jesus?' 'Well,' she said, with much emotion, 'I, I will try to be.' I laid hold of her hand, and said, 'My dear soul, you are not going to tell me that you will try to believe my Lord Jesus! I cannot have such talk from you. It means blank unbelief. What has HE done that you should talk of Him in that way? Would you tell *me* that you would try to believe *me*? I know you would not treat me so rudely. You think me a true man, and so you believe me at once; and surely you cannot do less with my Lord Jesus.' Then with tears she exclaimed, 'Oh, sir, do pray for me!' To this I replied, 'I do not feel I can do anything of the kind. What can I ask the Lord Jesus to do for one who will not trust

Him? I see nothing to pray about. If you will believe Him, you shall be saved; and if you will not believe Him, I cannot ask Him to invent a new way to gratify your unbelief.' Then she said again, 'I will try to believe'; but I told her solemnly I would have none of her trying; for the message from the Lord did not mention 'trying', but said, 'Believe on the Lord Jesus Christ, and thou shalt be saved' (see Acts 16:31). I pressed upon her the great truth, that 'He that believeth on Him hath everlasting life'; and its terrible reverse – 'He that believeth not is condemned already, because he hath not believed in the name of the only-begotten Son of God' (John 3:18). I urged her to full faith in the once crucified but now ascended Lord, and the Holy Spirit there and then enabled her to trust. She most tenderly said, 'Oh, sir, I have been looking to my feelings, and this has been my mistake! Now I trust my soul with Jesus, and I am saved.' She found immediate peace through believing. There is no other way.

God has been pleased to make the necessities of life very simple matters. We must eat; and even a blind man can find the way to his mouth. We must drink; and even the tiniest babe knows how to do this without instruction. We have a fountain in the grounds of the Stockwell Orphanage, and when it is running in the hot weather, the boys go to it naturally. We have no class for fountain-drill. Many poor boys have come to the Orphanage, but never one who was so ignorant that he did not know how to drink. Now faith is, in spiritual things, what eating and drinking are in temporal things. By the mouth of faith we take the blessings of grace into our spiritual nature, and they are ours. O you who would believe, but think you cannot, do

you not see that, as one can drink without strength, and as one can eat without strength, and gets strength by eating, so we may receive Jesus without effort, and by accepting Him we receive power for all such further effort as we may be called to put forth?

Faith is so simple a matter that, whenever I try to explain it, I am very fearful lest I should becloud its simplicity. When

Thomas Scott had printed his notes upon 'The Pilgrim's Progress', he asked one of his parishioners whether she understood the book. 'Oh yes, sir,' said she, 'I understand Mr Bunyan well enough, and I am hoping that one day, by divine grace, I may understand your explanations.' Should I not feel mortified if my reader should know what faith is, and then get confused by my explanation? I will, however, make one trial, and pray the Lord to make it clear.

I am told that on a certain highland road there was a disputed right of way. The owner wished to preserve his supremacy, and at the same time he did not wish to inconvenience the public: hence an arrangement which occasioned the following incident. Seeing a sweet country girl standing at the gate, a tourist went up to her, and offered her a shilling to permit him to pass. 'No, no,' said the child, 'I must not take anything from you; but you are to say, '*Please allow me to pass,*' and then you may come through and welcome.' The permission was to be asked for; but it could be had for the asking. Just so, eternal life is free; and it can be had, yea, it shall be at once had, by trusting in the Word of Him who cannot lie. Trust Christ, and by that trust you grasp salvation and eternal life. Do not philosophise. Do not sit down, and bother your poor brain. Just believe Jesus as you would believe your father. Trust Him as you trust your money with a banker, or your health with a doctor.

Faith will not long seem a difficulty to you; nor ought it to be so, for it is simple.

Faith is trusting, trusting wholly upon the person, work, merit, and power of the Son of God. Some think this trusting is a romantic business, but indeed it is the simplest thing that can possibly be. To some of us, truths which were once hard to believe are now matters of fact which we should find it hard to doubt. If one of our great grandfathers were to rise from the dead, and come into the present state of things, what a deal of trusting he would have to do! He would say tomorrow morning, 'Where are the flint and steel? I want a light'; and we should give him a little box with tiny pieces of wood in it, and tell him to strike one of them on the box. He would have to trust a good deal before he would believe that fire would thus be produced. We should next say to him, 'Now that you have a light, turn that tap, and light the gas.' He sees nothing. How can light come through an invisible vapour? And yet it does. 'Come with us, grandfather. Sit in that chair. Look at that box in front of you. You shall have your likeness directly.'

'No, child,' he would say, 'it is ridiculous. The sun take my portrait? I cannot believe it.' 'Yes, and you shall ride fifty miles in an hour without horses.' He will not believe it till we get him into the train. 'My dear sir, you shall speak to your son in New York, and he shall answer you in a few minutes.' Should we not astonish the old gentleman? Would he not want all his faith? Yet these things are believed by us without effort, because experience has made us familiar with them. But oh, how simple it is to us who have the new life, and have communion with spiritual realities! We have a Father to whom we speak, and He hears us, and a blessed Saviour who hears our heart's longings, and helps us in our struggles against sin. It is all plain to him that understandeth. May it now be plain to you!

5
FEARING TO BELIEVE

It is an odd product of our unhealthy nature – *the fear to believe*. Yet have I met with it often: so often that I wish I may never see it again. It looks like humility, and tries to pass itself off as the very soul of modesty, and yet it is an infamously proud thing: in fact, it is presumption playing the hypocrite. If men were afraid to *disbelieve*, there would be good sense in the fear; but to be afraid to trust their God is at best an absurdity, and in very deed it is a deceitful way of refusing to the Lord the honour that is due to His faithfulness and truth.

How unprofitable is the diligence which busies itself in finding out reasons why faith in our case should not be saving! We have God's word for it, that *whosoever believeth* in Jesus shall not perish, and we search for arguments why we should perish if we did believe. If any one gave me an estate, I certainly should not commence raising questions as to the title. What can be the use of inventing reasons why I should not hold my own house, or possess any other piece of property which is enjoyed by me? If the Lord is satisfied to save me through the merits of His dear Son, assuredly I may be satisfied to be so saved. If I take God at His word, the responsibility of fulfilling His promise does not lie with me, but with God, who made the promise.

But you fear that you may not be one of those for whom the promise is intended. Do not be alarmed by that idle suspicion. No soul ever came to Jesus wrongly. No one can come at all unless the Father draw him; and Jesus has said, 'Him that cometh to me I will in no wise cast out.' No soul ever lays hold on Christ in a way of robbery; he that hath Him hath Him of right divine; for the Lord's giving of Himself *for* us, and *to* us, is so free, that every soul that takes Him has a grace-given right to do so. If you lay hold on Jesus by the hem of His garment, without leave, and behind Him, yet virtue will flow from Him to you as surely as if He had called you out by name, and bidden you trust Him. Dismiss all fear when you trust the Saviour. Take Him and welcome. He that believeth in Jesus is one of God's elect.

Did you suggest that it would be a horrible thing if you were to trust in Jesus and yet perish? It would be so. But as you must perish if you do not trust, the risk at the worst is not very great.

I can but perish if I go;
I am resolved to try;
For if I stay away, I know
I must forever die.

Suppose you stand in the Slough of Depsond for ever; what will be the good of that? Surely it would be better to die struggling along the King's highway towards the Celestial City, than sinking deeper and deeper in the mire and filth of dark distrustful thoughts! You have nothing to lose, for you have lost everything already; therefore make a dash for it, and dare to believe in the mercy of God to you, even to you.

But one moans, 'What if I come to Christ, and He refuses me?' My answer is, 'Try Him.' You will be the first against

whom He has shut the door of hope. Friend, don't cross that bridge till you come to it! When Jesus casts you out, it will be time enough to despair; but that time will never come. 'This man receiveth sinners': He has not so much as begun to cast them out.

Have you never heard of the man who lost his way one night, and came to the edge of a precipice, as he thought, and in his own apprehension fell over the cliff? He clutched at an old tree, and there hung, clinging to his frail support with all his might. He felt persuaded that, should he quit his hold, he would be dashed in pieces on some awful rocks that waited for him down below. There he hung, with the sweat upon his brow, and anguish in every limb. He passed into a desperate state of fever and faintness, and at last his hands could hold up his body no longer. He relaxed his grasp! He dropped from his support! He fell – about a foot or so, and was received upon a soft mossy bank, whereon he lay, altogether unhurt, and perfectly safe till morning. Thus, in the darkness of their ignorance, many think that sure destruction awaits them, if they confess their sin, quit all hope in self, and resign themselves into the hands of God. They are afraid to quit the hope to which they ignorantly cling. It is an idle fear. Give up your hold upon everything but Christ, and drop. Drop from all trust in your works, or prayers, or feelings. Drop at once! Drop now! Soft and safe shall be the bank that receives you. Jesus Christ, in His love, in the efficacy of His precious blood, in His perfect righteousness, will give you immediate rest and peace. Cease from self-confidence. Fall into the arms of Jesus. This is the major part of faith – giving up every other hold, and simply falling upon Christ. There is no reason to fear: only ignorance causes your dread of that which will be your eternal safety. The death of carnal hope is the life of faith, and the life of faith is life everlasting. Let self die, that Christ may live in you.

But the mischief is that, to the one act of faith in Jesus, we cannot bring men. They will adopt any expedient sooner than have done with self. They fight shy of believing, and fear faith as if it were a monster. O foolish tremblers, who has bewitched you? You fear that which would be the death of all your fear, and the beginning of your joy. Why will you perish through perversely preferring other ways to God's own appointed plan of salvation?

Alas! there are many, many souls that say, 'We are bidden to trust in Jesus, but instead of that we will attend the means of grace regularly.' Attend public worship by all means, but not as a substitute for faith, or it will become a vain confidence. The command is, 'Believe and live';

attend to that, whatever else you do. 'Well, I shall take to reading good books; perhaps I shall get good that way.' Read the good books by all means, but that is not the gospel: the gospel is, 'Believe in the Lord Jesus Christ, and thou shalt be saved.' Suppose a physician has a patient under his care, and he says to him, 'You are to take a bath in the morning; it will be of very great service to your disease.' But the man takes a cup of tea in the morning instead of a bath, and he says, 'That will do as well, I have no doubt.' What does his physician say when he enquires – 'Did you follow my rule?' 'No, I did not.' 'Then you do not expect, of course, that there will be any good result from my visits, since you take no notice of my directions.' So we, practically, say to Jesus Christ, when we are under searching of soul, 'Lord, Thou badest me trust Thee, but I would sooner do something else! Lord, I want to have horrible convictions; I want to be shaken over hell's mouth; I want to be alarmed and distressed!' Yes, you want anything but what Christ prescribes for you, which is that you should *simply trust Him*. Whether you feel or do not feel, cast yourself on Him, that *He* may save you, and He alone. 'But you do not mean to say that you speak against praying, and reading good books, and so on?' Not one single word do I speak against any of those things, any more than, if I were the physician I quoted, I should speak against the man's drinking a cup of tea. Let him drink his tea; but not if he drinks it instead of taking the bath which is prescribed for him. So let the man pray: the more the better. Let the man search the Scriptures; but, remember, that if these things are put in the place of simple faith in Christ, the soul will be ruined. Beware lest it be said of any of you by our Lord, 'Ye search the Scriptures, for in them ye think ye have eternal life; but ye will not come unto Me that ye might have life.'

Come by faith to Jesus, for without Him you perish for ever. Did you ever notice how a fir-tree will get a hold among rocks which seem to afford it no soil? It sends a rootlet into any little crack which opens; it clutches even the bare rock as with a huge bird's claw; it holds fast, and binds itself to earth with a hundred anchorages. We have often seen trees thus firmly rooted upon detached masses of bare rock. Now, dear heart, let this be a picture of yourself. Grip the Rock of Ages. With the rootlet of little-faith hold to Him. Let that tiny feeler grow; and, meanwhile, send out another to take a new grasp of the same Rock. Lay hold on Jesus, and keep hold on Jesus. Grow up into Him. Twist the roots of your nature, the fibres of your heart, about Him. He is as free to you as the rocks are to the fir-tree: be you as firmly lashed to Him as the pine is to the mountain's side.

6
DIFFICULTY IN THE WAY OF BELIEVING

It may be that the reader feels a difficulty in believing. Let him consider. We cannot believe by an immediate act. The state of mind which we describe as believing is a result, following upon certain former states of mind. We come to faith by degrees. There may be such a thing as faith at first sight; but usually we reach faith by stages: we become interested, we consider, we hear evidence, we are convinced, and so led to believe. If, then, I wish to believe, but for some reason or other find that I cannot attain to faith, what shall I do? Shall I stand like a cow staring at a new gate; or shall I, like an intelligent being, use the proper means? If I wish to believe anything, what shall I do? We will answer according to the rules of common sense.

If I were told that the Sultan of Zanzibar was a good man, and it happened to be a matter of interest to me, I do not suppose I should feel any difficulty in believing it. But if for some reason I had a doubt about it, and yet wished to believe the news, how should I act? Should I not hunt up all the information within my reach about his Majesty, and try, by study of the newspapers and other documents, to arrive at the truth? Better still, if he happened to be in this country, and would see me, and I could also converse with members of his court, and citizens of his country,

I should be greatly helped to arrive at a decision by using these sources of information. Evidence weighed and knowledge obtained lead up to faith. It is true that faith in Jesus is the gift of God; but yet He usually bestows it in accordance with the laws of mind, and hence we are told that 'faith cometh by hearing, and hearing by the Word of God' (Rom. 10:17). If you want to believe in Jesus, hear about Him, read about Him, think about Him, know about Him, and so you will find faith springing up in your heart, like the wheat which comes up through the moisture and the heat operating upon the seed which has been sown. If I wished to have faith in a certain physician, I should ask for testimonials of his cures, I should wish to see the diplomas which certified to his professional knowledge, and I should also like to hear what he has to say upon certain complicated cases. In fact, I should take any means to know, in order that I might believe.

Be much in *hearing* concerning Jesus. Souls by hundreds come to faith in Jesus under a ministry which sets Him forth clearly and constantly. Few remain unbelieving under a preacher whose great subject is Christ crucified. Hear no minister of any other sort. There are such. I have heard of one who found in his pulpit Bible a paper bearing this text, '*Sir, we would see Jesus*'. Go to the place of worship to see Jesus; and if you cannot even hear the mention of His name, take yourself off to another place where He is more thought of, and is therefore more likely to be present.

Be much in *reading* about the Lord Jesus. The books of Scripture are the lilies among which He feedeth. The Bible is the window through which we may look and see our

Lord. Read over the story of His sufferings and death with devout attention, and before long the Lord will cause faith secretly to enter your soul. The Cross of Christ not only rewards faith, but begets faith. Many a believer can say –

> When I view Thee, wounded, grieving,
> Breathless, on the cursed tree,
> Soon I feel my heart believing
> Thou has suffered thus for me.

If hearing and reading suffice not, then deliberately *set your mind to work to overhaul the matter*, and have it out. Either believe, or know the reason why you do not believe. See the matter through to the utmost of your ability, and pray God to help you to make a thorough investigation, and to come to an honest decision one way or the other. Consider who Jesus was, and whether the constitution of His Person does not entitle Him to confidence. Consider what He did, and whether this also must not be good ground for trust. Consider Him as dying, rising from the dead, ascending, and ever living to intercede for transgressors; and see whether this does not entitle Him to be relied on by you. Then cry to Him, and see if He does not hear you. When Usher wished to know whether Rutherford was indeed as holy a man as he was said to be, he went to his house as a beggar, and gained a lodging, and heard the man of God pouring out his heart before the Lord in the night. If you would know Jesus, get as near to Him as you can by studying His character, and appealing to His love.

At one time I might have needed evidence to make me believe in the Lord Jesus; but now I know Him so well, by proving Him, that I should need a very great deal of evidence to make me doubt Him. It is now more natural to me to trust than to disbelieve: this is the new nature triumphing; it was not so at the first. The novelty of faith is, in the beginning, a source of weakness; but act after act of trusting turns faith into a habit. Experience brings to faith strong confirmation.

I am not perplexed with doubt, because the truth which I believe has wrought a miracle on me. By its means I have received and still retain a new life, to which I was once a stranger: and this is confirmation of the strongest sort. I am like the good man and his wife who had kept a lighthouse for years. A visitor, who came to see the lighthouse, looking out from the window over the waste of waters, asked the good woman, 'Are you not afraid at night, when the storm is out, and the big waves dash right over the lantern? Do you not fear that the lighthouse, and

all that is in it, will be carried away? I am sure I should be afraid to trust myself in a slender tower in the midst of the great billows.' The woman remarked that the idea never occurred to her now. She had lived there so long that she felt as safe on the lone rock as ever she did when she lived on the mainland. As for her husband, when asked if he did not feel anxious when the wind blew a hurricane, he answered, 'Yes, I feel anxious to keep the lamps well trimmed, and the light burning, lest any vessel should be wrecked.' As to anxiety about the safety of the lighthouse, or his own personal security in it, he had outlived all that. Even so it is with the full-grown believer. He can humbly say, 'I know whom I have believed, and am persuaded that He is able to keep that which I have committed unto

Him against that day.' From henceforth let no man trouble me with doubts and questionings; I bear in my soul the proofs of the Spirit's truth and power, and I will have none of your artful reasonings. The gospel to me is truth: I am content to perish if it be not true. I risk my soul's eternal fate upon the truth of the gospel, and I know that there is no risk in it. My one concern is to keep the lights burning, that I may thereby benefit others. Only let the Lord give me oil enough to feed my lamp, so that I may cast a ray across the dark and treacherous sea of life, and I am well content.

Now, troubled seeker, if it be so, that your minister, and many others in whom you confide, have found perfect peace and rest in the gospel, why should not you? Is the Spirit of the Lord straitened? Do not His words do good to them that walk uprightly? Will not you also try their saving virtue?

Most true is the gospel, for God is its Author. Believe it. Most able is the Saviour, for He is the Son of God. Trust Him. Most powerful is His precious blood. Look to it for pardon. Most loving is His gracious heart. Run to it at once.

Thus would I urge the reader to seek faith; but if he be unwilling, what more can I do? I have brought the horse to the water, but I cannot make him drink. This, however, be it remembered – *unbelief is wilful when evidence is put in a man's way, and he refuses carefully to examine it.* He that does not desire to know, and accept the truth, has himself to thank if he dies with a lie in his right hand. It is true that 'he that believeth and is baptised shall be saved': it is equally true that 'he that believeth not shall be damned' (see Mark 16:16).

7
A HELPFUL SURVEY

To help the seeker to a true faith in Jesus, I would remind him of the work of the Lord Jesus in the room and place and stead of sinners. 'When we were yet without strength, in due time *Christ died for the ungodly*' (Rom. 5:6). 'Who His own self bare our sins in His own body on the tree' (1 Pet. 2:24). 'The Lord hath laid on Him the iniquity of us all' (Isa. 53:6). 'For Christ also hath once suffered for sins, the Just for the unjust, that He might bring us to God' (1 Pet. 3:18).

Upon one declaration of Scripture let the reader fix his eye. '*With His stripes we are healed*' (Isa. 53:5). God here treats sin as a disease, and He sets before us the costly remedy which He has provided.

I ask you very solemnly to accompany me in your meditations, for a few minutes, while I bring before you the stripes of the Lord Jesus. The Lord resolved to restore us, and therefore He sent His only-begotten Son, 'very God of very God', that He might descend into this world to take upon Himself our nature, in order to our redemption. He lived as a man among men; and, in due time, after thirty years or more of obedience, the time came when He should do us the greatest service of all, namely, stand in our stead, and bear 'the chastisement of our peace' (Isa. 53:5). He went to Gethsemane, and there, at the first taste of our bitter cup, He sweat great drops of blood. He went to Pilate's hall, and Herod's judgment seat, and there drank draughts of pain and scorn in our room and place. Last of all, they took Him to the cross, and nailed Him there to die – to die in our stead. The word 'stripes' is used to set forth His sufferings, both of body and of soul. The whole of Christ was made a sacrifice for us: His whole manhood suffered. As to His body, it shared with His mind in a grief that never can be described. In the beginning of His passion, when He emphatically suffered instead of us, He was in an agony, and from His bodily frame a bloody sweat distilled so copiously as to fall to the ground. It is very rarely that a man sweats blood. There have been one or two instances of it, and they have been followed by almost immediate death; but our Saviour lived – lived after an agony which, to anyone else, would have proved fatal. Ere He could cleanse His face from this dreadful crimson, they hurried Him to the high priest's hall. In the dead of night they bound Him, and led Him away. Anon they took Him to Pilate and to Herod. These scourged Him, and their soldiers spat on His face, and buffeted Him, and put on His head a crown of thorns. Scourging is one of the most awful tortures that can be inflicted by malice. It was formerly the disgrace of the British army that the 'cat' was used upon the soldier: a brutal infliction of torture. But to the Roman, cruelty was so natural that he made his common punishments worse than brutal. The Roman scourge is said to have been made of the sinews of oxen, twisted into knots, and into these knots were inserted slivers of bone, and huckle-bones of sheep; so that every time the scourge fell upon the bare back, 'the plowers made deep furrows'. Our Saviour was called upon to endure the fierce pain of the Roman scourge, and this not as the *finis* of His punishment, but as a preface to crucifixion. To this His persecutors added buffeting, and plucking of the hair: they spared Him no form of pain. In all His faintness, through bleeding and fasting, they made Him carry His cross until another was forced, by the forethought of their cruelty, to bear it, lest their victim should die on the road. They stripped Him, and threw Him down, and nailed Him to the wood. They pierced His hands and His feet. They lifted up the tree, with Him upon it, and then dashed it down into its place in the ground, so that all His limbs were dislocated, according to the lament of the twenty-second psalm, 'I am poured out like water, and all my bones are out of joint.' He hung in the burning sun till the fever dissolved His strength, and He said, 'My heart is like wax; it is melted in the midst of my bowels. My strength is dried up like a potsherd; and my tongue cleaveth to my jaws; and thou hast brought me into the dust of death' (Ps. 22:14-15). There He hung, a spectacle to God and men. The weight of His body was first sustained by His feet, till the nails tore through the tender nerves: and then the painful load began to drag upon His hands, and rend those sensitive parts of His frame. How small a wound in the hand has brought on lockjaw! How awful must have been the torment caused by that dragging iron tearing through the delicate parts of the hands and feet! Now were all manner of bodily pains centred in His tortured frame. All the while His enemies stood around, pointing at

Him in scorn, thrusting out their tongues in mockery, jesting at His prayers, and gloating over His sufferings. He cried, 'I thirst' (John 19:28), and then they gave Him vinegar mingled with gall. After a while He said, 'It is finished' (John 19:30). He had endured the utmost of appointed grief, and had made full vindication to divine justice: then, and not till then, He gave up the ghost. Holy men of old have enlarged most lovingly upon the bodily sufferings of our Lord, and I have no hesitation in doing the same, trusting that trembling sinners may see salvation in these painful 'stripes' of the Redeemer.

To describe the outward sufferings of our Lord is not easy: I acknowledge that I have failed. But His soul-sufferings, which were the soul of His sufferings, who can even conceive, much less express, what they were? At the very first I told you that He sweat great drops of blood. That was His heart driving out its life-floods to the surface through the terrible depression of spirit which was upon Him. He said, 'My soul is exceeding sorrowful, even unto death' (Matt. 26:38). The betrayal by Judas, and the desertion of the twelve, grieved our Lord; but the weight of our sin was the real pressure on His heart. Our guilt was the olive-press which forced from Him the moisture of His life. No language can ever tell His agony in prospect of His passion; how little then can we conceive the passion itself? When nailed to the cross, He endured what no martyr ever suffered; for martyrs, when they have died, have been so sustained of God that they have rejoiced amid their pain; but our Redeemer was forsaken of His Father, until He cried, 'My God, my God, why hast Thou forsaken me?' (Matt. 27:46). That was the bitterest cry of all, the utmost depth of His unfathomable grief. Yet was it needful that He should be deserted, because God must turn His back on sin, and consequently upon Him who was made sin for us. The soul of the great Substitute suffered a horror of misery instead of that horror of hell into which sinners would have been plunged had He not taken their sin upon Himself, and been made a curse for them. It is written, 'Cursed is every one that hangeth on a tree' (Gal. 3:13); but who knows what that curse means?

The remedy for your sins and mine is found in the sub-stitutionary sufferings of the Lord Jesus, and in these only. These 'stripes' of the Lord Jesus Christ were on our behalf. Do you enquire, 'Is there anything for us to do, to remove the guilt of sin?' I answer: There is nothing whatever for you to do. By the stripes of Jesus we are healed. All those stripes He has endured, and left not one of them for us to bear.

'But must we not believe on Him?' Ay, certainly. If I say of a certain ointment that it heals, I do not deny that you need a bandage with which to apply it to the wound. Faith is the linen which binds the plaster of Christ's reconciliation to the sore of our sin. The linen does not heal: that is the work of the ointment. So faith does not heal: that is the work of the atonement of Christ.

'But we must repent,' cries another. Assuredly we must, and shall, for repentance is the first sign of healing: but the stripes of Jesus heal us, and not our repentance. These stripes, when applied to the heart, work repentance in us: we hate sin because it made Jesus suffer.

When you intelligently trust in Jesus as having suffered for you, then you discover the fact that God will never punish you for the same offence for which Jesus died. His justice will not permit Him to see the debt paid, first, by the Surety, and then again by the debtor. Justice cannot twice demand a recompense: if my bleeding Surety has borne my guilt, then I cannot bear it. Accepting Christ Jesus as suffering for me, I have accepted a complete discharge from judicial liability. I have been condemned in Christ, and there is, therefore, now no condemnation to me any more. This is the ground-work of the security of the sinner who believes in Jesus: he lives because Jesus died in his room, and place, and stead; and he is acceptable before God because Jesus is accepted. The person for whom Jesus is an accepted Substitute must go free; none can touch him; he is clear. O my hearer, will you have Jesus Christ to be your Substitute? If so, thou art free. 'He that believeth on Him is not condemned' (John 3:18). Thus 'with His stripes we are healed' (Isa. 53:5).

8
A REAL HINDRANCE

Although it is by no means a difficult thing in itself to believe Him who cannot lie, and to trust in One whom we know to be able to save, yet something may intervene which may render even this a hard thing to my reader. That hindrance may be a secret, and yet it may be none the less real. A door may be closed, not by a great stone which all can see, but by an invisible bolt which shoots into a holdfast quite out of sight. A man may have good eyes, and yet may not be able to see an object, because another substance comes in the way. You could not even see the sun if a handkerchief, or a mere piece of rag, were tied over your face. Oh, the bandages which men persist in binding over their own eyes!

A sweet sin, harboured in the heart, will prevent a soul from laying hold upon Christ by faith. The Lord Jesus has come to save us from sinning; and if we are resolved to go on sinning, Christ and our souls will never agree. If a man takes poison, and a doctor is called in to save his life, he may have a sure antidote ready; but if the patient persists in keeping the poison-bottle at his lips, and will continue to swallow the deadly drops, how can the doctor save him? Salvation consists largely in parting the sinner from his sin, and the very nature of salvation would have to be changed before we could speak of a man's being saved when he is loving sin, and wilfully living in it. A man cannot be made white, and yet continue black; he cannot be healed, and yet remain sick; neither can anyone be saved, and be still a lover of evil.

A drunkard will be saved by believing in Christ – that is to say, he will be saved from being a drunkard; but if he determines still to make himself intoxicated, he is not saved from it, and he has not truly believed in Jesus. A liar can by faith be saved from falsehood, but then he leaves off lying, and is careful to speak the truth. Anyone can see with half an eye that he cannot be saved from being a liar, and yet go on in his old style of deceit and untruthfulness. A person who is at enmity with another will be saved from that feeling of enmity by believing in the Lord Jesus; but if he vows that he will still cherish the feeling of hate, it is clear that he is not saved from it, and equally clear that he has not believed in the Lord Jesus unto salvation. The great matter is to be delivered from the love of sin: this is the sure effect of trust in the Saviour; but if this effect is so far from being desired that it is even refused, all talk of trusting in the Saviour for salvation is an idle tale. A man goes to the shipping-office, and asks if he can be taken to America. He is assured that a ship is just ready, and that he has only to go on board, and he will soon reach New York. 'But,' says he, 'I want to stop at home in England, and mind my shop all the time I am crossing the Atlantic.' The agent thinks he is talking to a madman, and tells him to go about his business, and not waste his time by playing the fool. To pretend to trust Christ to save you from sin while you are still determined to continue in it, is making a mock of

Christ. I pray my reader not to be guilty of such profanity. Let him not dream that the holy Jesus will be the patron of iniquity.

Do you see the tree in my picture? The ivy has grown all over it, and is strangling it, sucking out its life, and killing it. Can that tree be saved? The gardener thinks it can be. He is willing to do his best. But before he begins to use his axe and his knife, he is told that he must not cut away the ivy. 'Ah! then,' he says, 'it is impossible. It is the ivy which is killing the tree, and if you want the tree saved, you cannot save the ivy. If you trust me to preserve the tree, you must let me get the deadly climber away from it.' Is not that common sense? Certainly it is. You do not trust the tree to the gardener unless you trust him to cut away that which is deadly to it. If the sinner will keep his sin, he must die in it; if he is willing to be rescued from his sin, the Lord Jesus is able to do it, and will do it if he commits his case to His care.

What, then, is your darling sin? Is it any gross wrongdoing? Then very shame should make you cease from it. Is it love of the world, or fear of men, or longing for evil gains? Surely, none of these things should reconcile you to living in enmity with God, and beneath His frown. Is it human love, which is eating like a canker into the heart? Can any creature rival the Lord Jesus? Is it not idolatry to allow any earthly thing to compare for one instant with the Lord God? 'Well,' said one, 'for me to give up the particular sin by which I am held captive, would be to my serious injury in business, would ruin my prospects, and lessen my usefulness in many ways.' If it be so, you have your case met by the words of the Lord Jesus, who bids you to pluck out your eye, and cut off your hand or foot, and cast it from you, rather than be cast into hell. It is better to enter into life with one eye, with the poorest prospects, than to keep all your hopes, and be out of Christ. Better be a lame believer than a leaping sinner. Better be in the rear rank of life in the army of Christ than lead the van and be a chief officer under the command of Satan. If you win Christ, it will little matter what you lose. No doubt many have had to suffer that which has maimed and lamed them for this life; but if they have entered thereby into eternal life, they have been great gainers.

It comes to this, my friend, as it did with John Bunyan; a voice now speaks to you, and says –

WILT THOU KEEP THY SIN AND GO TO HELL?
OR
LEAVE THY SIN AND GO TO HEAVEN?

The point should be decided before you quit the spot. In the name of God, I ask you, Which shall it be? – Christ and salvation, or the favourite sin and damnation? There is no middle course. Waiting or refusing to decide will practically be a sure decision for the evil one. He that stands questioning whether he will be honest or not, is already out of the straight line: he that does not know whether he wishes to be cleansed from sin gives evidence of a foul heart.

If you are anxious to give up every evil way, our Lord Jesus will enable you to do so at once. His grace has already changed the direction of your desires: in fact, your heart is renewed. Therefore, rest on Him to strengthen you to battle with temptations as they arise, and to fulfil the Lord's commands from day to day. The Lord Jesus is great at making the lame man to leap like a hart, and in enabling those who are sick of the palsy to take up their bed and walk. He will make you able to conquer the evil habit. He will even cast the devil out of you. Yes, if you had seven devils, He could drive them out at once; there is no limit to His power to cleanse and sanctify. Now that you are willing to be made whole, the great difficulty is removed. He that has set the will right can arrange all your other powers, and make them move to His praise. You would not have earnestly desired to quit all sin if He had not secretly inclined you in that direction. If you now trust Him, it will be clear that He has begun a good work in you, and we feel assured that He will carry it on.

9
ON RAISING QUESTIONS

In these days, a simple, childlike faith is very rare; but the usual thing is to believe nothing, and question everything. Doubts are as plentiful as blackberries, and all hands and lips are stained with them. To me it seems very strange that men should hunt up difficulties as to their own salvation. If I were doomed to die, and I had a hint of mercy, I am sure I should not set my wits to work to find out reasons why I should not be pardoned. I could leave my enemies to do that: I should be on the look-out in a very different direction. If I were drowning, I should sooner catch a straw than push a life-belt away from me. To reason against one's own life is a sort of constructive suicide of which only a drunken man would be guilty. To argue against your only hope is like a foolish man sitting on a bough, and chopping it away so as to let himself down. Who but an idiot would do that? Yet many appear to be special pleaders for their own ruin. They hunt the Bible through for threatening texts; and when they have done with that, they turn to reason, and philosophy, and scepticism, in order to shut the door in their own faces. Surely this is poor employment for a sensible man.

Many nowadays who cannot quite get away from religious thought, are able to stave off the inconvenient pressure of conscience by quibbling over the great truths of revelation. Great mysteries are in the Book of God of

necessity; for how can the infinite God so speak that all His thoughts can be grasped by finite man? But it is the height of folly to get discussing these deep things, and to leave plain, soul-saving truths in abeyance. It reminds one of the two philosophers who debated about food, and went away empty from the table, while the common countryman in the corner asked no question, but used his knife and fork with great diligence, and went on his way rejoicing. Thousands are now happy in the Lord through receiving the gospel like little children; while others, who can always see difficulties, or invent them, are as far off as ever from any comfortable hope of salvation. I know many very decent people who seem to have resolved never to come to Christ till they can understand how the doctrine of election is consistent with the free invitations of the gospel. I might just as well determine never to eat a morsel of bread till it has been explained to me how it is that God keeps me alive, and yet I must eat to live. The fact is, that we most of us *know* quite enough already, and the real want with us is not light in the head, but truth in the heart; not help over difficulties, but grace to make us hate sin and seek reconciliation.

Here let me add a warning against tampering with the Word of God. No habit can be more ruinous to the soul. It is cool, contemptuous impertinence to sit down and correct your Maker, and it tends to make the heart harder than the nether millstone. We remember one who used a penknife on his Bible, and it was not long before he had given up all his former beliefs. The spirit of reverence is healthy, but the impertinence of criticising the inspired Word is destructive of all proper feeling towards God.

If ever a man does feel his need of a Saviour after treating Scripture with a proud, critical spirit, he is very apt to find his conscience standing in the way, and hindering him from comfort by reminding him of ill-treatment of the sacred Word. It comes hard to him to draw consolation out of passages of the Bible which he has treated cavalierly,

or even set aside altogether, as unworthy of consideration. In his distress the sacred texts seem to laugh at his calamity. When the time of need comes, the wells which he stopped with stones yield no water for his thirst. Beware, when you despise a Scripture, lest you cast away the only friend that can help you in the hour of agony.

A certain German duke was accustomed to call upon his servant to read a chapter of the Bible to him every morning. When anything did not square with his judgment he would sternly cry, 'Hans, strike that out.' At length Hans was a long time before he began to read. He fumbled over the Book, till his master called out, 'Hans, why do you not read?' Then Hans answered, 'Sir, there is hardly anything left. It is all struck out!' One day his master's objections had one way, and another day they had taken another turn, and another set of passages had been blotted, till nothing was left to instruct or comfort him. Let us not, by carping criticism, destroy our own

mercies. We may yet need those promises which appear needless; and those portions of Holy Writ which have been most assailed by sceptics may yet prove essential to our very life: wherefore let us guard the priceless treasure of the Bible, and determine never to resign a single line of it.

What have we to do with recondite questions while our souls are in peril? The way to escape from sin is plain enough. The wayfaring man, though a fool, shall not err therein. God has not mocked us with a salvation which we cannot understand. BELIEVE AND LIVE is a command which a babe may comprehend and obey.

Doubt no more, but now believe;
Question not, but just receive.
Artful doubts and reasonings be
Nailed with Jesus to the tree.

Instead of cavilling at Scripture, the man who is led of the Spirit of God will close in with the Lord Jesus at once. Seeing that thousands of decent, common-sense people – people, too, of the best character – are trusting their all with Jesus, he will do the same, and have done with further delays. Then has he begun a life worth living, and he may have done with further fear. He may at once advance to that higher and better way of living, which grows out of love to Jesus, the Saviour. Why should not the reader do so at once? Oh that he would!

A Newark, New Jersey, butcher received a letter from his old home in Germany, notifying that he had, by the death of a relative, fallen heir to a considerable amount of money. He was cutting up a pig at the time. After reading

the letter, he hastily tore off his dirty apron, and did not stop to see the pork cut up into sausages, but left the shop to make preparations for going home to Germany. Do you blame him, or would you have had him stop in Newark with his block and his cleaver?

See here the operation of faith. The butcher believed what was told him, and acted on it at once. Sensible fellow, too!

God has sent His messages to man, telling him the good news of salvation. When a man believes the good news to be true, he accepts the blessing announced to him, and hastens to lay hold upon it. If he truly believes, he will at once take Christ, with all He has to bestow, turn from his present evil ways, and set out for the Heavenly City, where the full blessing is to be enjoyed. He cannot be holy too soon, or too early quit the ways of sin. If a man could really see what sin is, he would flee from it as from a deadly serpent, and rejoice to be freed from it by Christ Jesus.

10
WITHOUT FAITH NO SALVATION

Some think it hard that there should be nothing for them but ruin if they will not believe in Jesus Christ; but if you will think for a minute you will see that it is just and reasonable. I suppose there is no way for a man to keep his strength up except by eating. If you were to say, 'I will not eat again, I despise such animalism', you might go to Madeira, or travel in all lands (supposing you lived long enough!), but you would most certainly find that no climate and no exercise would avail to keep you alive if you refused food. Would you then complain, 'It is a hard thing that I should die because I do not believe in eating'? It is not an unjust thing that if you are so foolish as not to eat, you must die. It is precisely so with believing. 'Believe, and thou art saved'. If thou wilt not believe, it is no hard thing that thou shouldst be lost. It would be strange indeed if it were not to be the case.

A man who is thirsty stands before a fountain. 'No,' he says, 'I will never touch a drop of moisture as long as I live. Cannot I get my thirst quenched in my own way?' We tell him, no; he must drink or die. He says, 'I will never drink; but it is a hard thing that I must therefore die. It is a bigoted, cruel thing to tell me so.' He is wrong. His thirst is the inevitable result of neglecting a law of nature. You, too, must believe or die; why refuse to obey the command?

Drink, man, drink! Take Christ and live. There is the way of salvation, and to enter you must trust Christ; but there is nothing hard in the fact that you must perish if you will not trust the Saviour. Here is a man out at sea; he has a chart, and that chart, if well studied, will, with the help of the compass, guide him to his journey's end. The pole-star gleams out amidst the cloud-rifts, and that, too, will help him. 'No,' says he, 'I will have nothing to do with your stars; I do not believe in the North Pole. I shall not attend to that little thing inside the box; in your chart, and I will have nothing to do with it. The art of navigation is only a lot of nonsense, got up by people on purpose to make money, and I will not be gulled by it.' The man never reaches port, and he says it is a very hard thing – a very hard thing. I do not think so. Some of you say, 'I am not going to read the Scriptures; I am not going to listen to your talk about Jesus Christ: I do not believe in such things.' Then Jesus says, 'He that believeth not shall be damned.' 'That's very hard,' say you. But it is not so. It is not more hard than the fact that if you reject the compass and the pole-star you will not reach your port. There is no help for it; it must be so.

You say you will have nothing to do with Jesus and His blood, and you pooh-pooh all religion. You will find it hard to laugh these matters down when you come to die, when the clammy sweat must be wiped from your brow, and your heart beats against your ribs as if it wanted to leap out and fly away from God. O soul! you will find then, that those Sundays, and those services, and this old Book, are something more and better than you thought they were, and you will wonder that you were so simple as to neglect any true help to salvation. Above all, what woe it will be to have neglected Christ, that Pole-star which alone can guide the mariner to the haven of rest!

Where do you live?

You live, perhaps, on the other side of the river, and you have to cross a bridge before you can get home. You have been so silly as to nurse the notion that you do not believe in bridges, nor in boats, nor in the existence of such a thing as water. You say, 'I am not going over any of your bridges, and I shall not get into any of your boats. I do not believe that there is a river, or that there is any such stuff as water.' You are going home, and soon you come to the old bridge; but you will not cross it. Yonder is a boat; but you are determined that you will not get into it. There is the river, and you resolve that you will not cross it in the usual way; and yet you think it is very hard that you cannot get home. Surely something has destroyed your reasoning powers, for you would not think it so hard if you were in your senses. If a man will not do the thing that is necessary to a certain end, how can he expect to gain that end? You have taken poison, and the physician brings an antidote, and says, 'Take it quickly, or you will die; but if you take it quickly, I will guarantee that the poison will be neutralised.' But you say, 'No, doctor, I do not believe in antidotes. Let everything take its course; let every tub stand on its own bottom; I will have nothing to do with your remedy. Besides, I do not believe that there is any remedy for the poison I have taken; and, what is more, I don't care whether there is or not.'

Well, sir, you will die; and when the coroner's inquest is held on your body, the verdict will be, 'Served him right!' So will it be with you if, having heard the gospel of Jesus Christ, you say, 'I am too much of an advanced man to have anything to do with that old-fashioned notion of substitution. I shall not attend to the preacher's talk about sacrifice and blood-shedding.' Then, when you perish, the verdict given by your conscience, which will sit upon the King's quest at last, will run thus, '*Suicide: he destroyed his own soul.*' So says the old Book – 'O Israel, thou hast destroyed thyself!' (Hosea 13:9). Reader, I implore thee, do not so.

11
TO THOSE WHO HAVE BELIEVED

Friends, if now you have begun to trust the Lord, trust Him out and out. Let your faith be the most real and practical thing in your whole life. Don't trust the Lord in mere sentiment about a few great spiritual things; but trust Him for everything, for ever, both for time and eternity, for body and for soul. See how the Lord hangeth the world upon nothing but His own word! It has neither prop nor pillar. Yon great arch of heaven stands without a buttress or a wooden centre. The Lord can and will bear all the strain that faith can ever put upon Him. The greatest troubles are easy to His power, and the darkest mysteries are clear to His wisdom. Trust God up to the hilt. Lean, and lean hard;

yes, lean all your weight, and every other weight upon the Mighty God of Jacob.

The future you can safely leave with the Lord, who ever liveth and changeth. The past is now in your Saviour's hand, and you shall never be condemned for it, whatever it may have been, for the Lord has cast your iniquities into the midst of the sea. Believe at this moment in your present privileges. *You are saved.* If you are a believer in the Lord Jesus, you have passed from death unto life, and *you are saved.* In the old slave days a lady brought her black servant on board an English ship, and she laughingly said to the Captain, 'I suppose if I and Aunt Chloe were to go to England she would be free?' 'Madam,' said the Captain, 'she is *now* free. The moment she came on board a British vessel she was free.' When the negro woman knew this, she did not leave the ship – not she. It was not *the hope of liberty* that made her bold, but *the fact of liberty.* So you are not now merely hoping for eternal life, but '*He that believeth in Him hath everlasting life.*' Accept this as a fact revealed in the sacred Word, and begin to rejoice accordingly. Do not reason about it, or call it in question; believe it, and leap for joy.

I want my reader, upon believing in the Lord Jesus, to believe for *eternal* salvation. Do not be content with the notion that you can receive a new birth which will die out, a heavenly life which will expire, a pardon which will be recalled. The Lord Jesus gives to His sheep *eternal* life, and do not be at rest until you have it. Now, if it be eternal, how can it die out? Be saved out and out, for eternity. There is 'a living and incorruptible seed, which liveth and abideth for ever' (see 1 Pet. 1:23); do not be put off with a temporary change, a sort of grace which will only bloom to fade. You are now starting on the railway of grace – *take a ticket all the way through*. I have no commission to preach to you salvation for a time: the gospel I am bidden to set before you is, 'He that believeth and is baptised shall be saved' (see Mark 16:16). He shall be saved from sin, from going back to sin, from turning aside to the broad road. May the Holy Spirit lead you to believe for nothing less than that. 'Do you mean,' says one, 'that I am to believe if I once trust Christ I shall be saved whatever sin I may choose to commit?' I have never said anything of the kind. I have described true salvation as a thorough change of heart of so radical a kind that it will alter your tastes and desires; and I say that if you have such a change wrought in you by the Holy Spirit, it will be permanent; for the Lord's work is not like the cheap work of the present day, which soon goes to pieces. Trust the Lord to keep you, however long you may live, and however much you may be tempted; and 'according to your faith, so be it unto you' (see Matt. 9:29). Believe in Jesus for *everlasting* life.

Oh, that you may also trust the Lord for all the sufferings of this present time! In the world you will have tribulation; learn by faith to know that all things work together for good, and then submit yourself to the Lord's will. Look at the sheep when it is being shorn. If it lies quite still, the shears will not hurt it; if it struggles, or even shrinks, it may be pricked. Submit yourselves under the hand of God, and affliction will lose its sharpness. Self-will and repining

cause us a hundred times more grief than our afflictions themselves. So believe your Lord as to be certain that His will must be far better than yours, and therefore you not only submit to it, but even rejoice in it.

Trust the Lord Jesus in the matter of *sanctification*. Certain friends appear to think that the Lord Jesus cannot sanctify them wholly, spirit, soul, and body. Hence they willingly give way to such and such sins under the notion that there is no help for it, but that they must pay tribute to the devil as long as they live in that particular form. Do not basely bow your neck in bondage to any sin, but strike hard for liberty. Be it anger, or unbelief, or sloth, or any other form of iniquity, we are able, by divine grace, to drive out the Canaanite, and, what is more, we must drive him out. No virtue is impossible to him that believeth in Jesus, and no sin need have victory over him. Indeed, it is written, 'Sin shall not have dominion over you: for ye are not under the law, but under grace'. Believe for high degrees of joy in the Lord, and likeness to Jesus, and advance to take full possession of these precious things; for as thou believest, so shall it be unto thee. 'All things are possible to him that believeth'; and he who is the chief of sinners may yet be not a whit behind the greatest of saints.

Often realise the joy of heaven. This is grand faith; and yet it is no more than we ought to have. Within a very short time the man who believes in the Lord Jesus shall be with Him where He is. This head will wear a crown; these eyes shall see the King in His beauty; these ears shall hear His own dear voice; this soul shall be in glory; and this poor body shall be raised from the dead and joined in incorruption to the perfected soul! Glory, glory, glory! And so near, so sure. Let us at once rehearse the music and anticipate the bliss!

But cries one, 'We are not there yet'. No: but faith fills us with delight in the blessed prospect, and meanwhile it sustains us on the road. Reader, I long that you may be a firm believer in the Lord alone. I want you to get wholly upon the rock, and not keep a foot on the sand. In this mortal life *trust God for all things*; and trust Him alone. This is the way to live. I know it by experience. God's bare arm is quite enough to lean upon. I will give you a bit of the experience of an old labouring man I once knew. He feared God above many, and was very deeply taught of the Spirit. He was great at hedging and ditching; but greater at simple trust. Here is how he described faith: 'It was a bitter winter, and I had no work, and no bread in the house. The children were crying. The snow was deep, and my way was dark. My old master told me I might have a bit of wood when I wanted it; so I thought a bit of fire would warm the poor children, and I went out with my chopper to get some fuel. I was standing near a deep ditch full of snow, which had drifted into it many feet deep – in fact, I did not know how deep. While aiming a blow at a bit of wood my bill-hook slipped out of my hand, and went right down into the snow, where I could not hope to find it. Standing there with no food, no fire, and the chopper gone, something seemed to say to me, "Will Richardson, can you trust God now?" and my very soul said, "That I can".' This is true faith – the faith which trusts the Lord when the bill-hook is gone: the faith which believes God when all outward appearances give Him the lie; the faith which is happy with God alone when all friends turn their backs upon you. Dear reader, may you and I have this precious faith, this real faith, this God-honouring faith! The Lord's truth deserves it; His love claims it, His faithfulness constrains it. Happy is He who has it! He is the man whom the Lord loves, and the world shall be made to know it before all is finished.

After all, the very best faith is an everyday faith: the faith which deals with bread and water, coats and stockings, children and cattle, house rent and weather. The superfine confectionery religion which is only available on Sundays, and in drawing-room meetings and Bible readings, will never take a soul to heaven till life becomes one long Conference, and there are seven Sabbaths in a week. Faith is doing her very best when for many years she plods on, month by month, trusting the Lord about the sick husband, the failing daughter, the declining business, the unconverted friend, and suchlike things.

Faith also helps us to use the world as not abusing it. It is good at hard work, and at daily duty. It is not an angelic thing for skies and stars, but a human grace, at home in kitchens and workshops. It is a sort of maid-of-all-work, and is at home at every kind of labour, and in every rank of life. It is a grace for every day, all the year round. Holy confidence in God is never out of work. Faith's ware is so valued at the heavenly court that she always has one fine piece of work or another on the wheel or in the furnace. Men dream that heroes are only to be made on special occasions, once or twice in a century; but in truth the finest heroes are home-spun, and are more often hidden in obscurity than platformed by public observation. Trust in the living God is the bullion out of which heroism is coined. Perseverance in well-doing is one of the fields in which faith grows not flowers, but the wheat of her harvest. Plodding on in hard work, bringing up a family on a few shillings a week, bearing constant pain with patience, and so forth – these are the feats of valour through which God is glorified by the rank and file of His believing people.

Reader, you and I will be of one mind in this: we will not pine to be great, but we will be eager to be good. For this we will rely upon the Lord our God, whose we are, and whom we serve. We will ask to be made holy throughout every day of the week. We will pray to our God as much about our daily business as about our soul's salvation. We will trust Him concerning our farm, and our turnips, and our cows, as well as concerning our spiritual privileges and our hope of heaven. The Lord Jehovah is our household God; Jesus is our brother born for adversity; and the Holy Spirit is our Comforter in every hour of trial. We have not an unapproachable God: He hears, He pities, He helps. Let us trust Him without a break, without a doubt, without a hesitation. The life of faith is life within God's wicket gate. If we have hitherto stood trembling outside in the wide world of unbelief, may the Holy Spirit enable us now to take the great decisive step, and say, once for all, 'Lord, I believe: help Thou mine unbelief!' (Mark 9:24).